Host a Successful Craft Fair

Tips for Top-Selling Events

Brenda DeHaan

First edition: December 2019
Updated in June 2024

DeHaan, Brenda
1. Crafts and hobbies. 2. Craft and vendor shows. 3.
Handicrafts. 4. Marketing.5. Fundraising. 6. How-to
manual.
745

Contents

Introduction

A craft fair serves a variety of purposes:

- fundraiser for an organization
- sales for the crafters and direct sales vendors
- community fellowship

Hosting a successful craft fair requires a lot of organization and work. It takes both emotional and physical energy. It takes a team to execute the event properly.

The purpose of this book is to make the process easier, especially if you do not have much experience with hosting craft fairs. The information is geared for smaller craft fairs held indoors, but many tips may also be applied to larger events.

For simplicity's sake, the term *craft fair* will be used to include various types of vendor events, not strictly fairs with only homemade crafts. Also, *you* will signify "you and your fellow committee members."

Vendors are there to make money and hope to have fun doing it. This is often a supplemental job, their time is limited, and they want positive results for their day supporting your cause.

The fair's sponsor receives a guaranteed income because of the vendors' booth fees. In addition, the host might have its own table of items for sale and/or a concession stand at the event. The vendors' sales rely on crowd attendance.

Communities have their own traditions and cultures. What works in one town may be a total dud in another. This book contains ideas to consider or revise for your event. Learning different ways to do things makes it easier to determine the best way for you and your team.

Make your craft fair special, one that people look forward to attending each year.

Vital for Success

Advertising is key to attendance.

Social media is a free way to spread the word, but it cannot be the *only* method. Not everyone has Facebook or other social media platforms. Of those who do, not everyone sees notifications of events like craft fairs.

Definitely utilize social media and invite your vendors to share the event on their pages. Make sure that the event's privacy setting is set to **public** for sharing and viewing.

Advertisements in the **area shopping guides** are essential. Some newspapers will publish a brief submitted article about your upcoming event if you purchase an ad. It doesn't have to be big; the ad just needs to include the basics of *what, when,* and *where.*

Ideally, publish a small ad 5-8 weeks in advance to solicit vendors, another one announcing the craft fair the week before the event, and then a bigger display ad the week of the fair. Advertisements matter. Shopping guides reach thousands of readers, and reading something printed often sticks in people's minds longer than skimming and scrolling online.

You want other communities to know about your show, so include small advertisements in shopping guides in adjoining areas. Some people read the classified ads better than the more expensive display ads.

PICKSTOWN'S 7TH ANNUAL

Fall Festival
& Craft Fair

Saturday, November 2nd
10 AM – 2 PM at the Rainbow Room

20+ Vendors

Lunch will be served. Come early
so you don't miss our "famous"
cheesy baked potato soup!

BAKE SALE
1PM, TUESDAY, NOVEMBER 26, 2019
FALL CRAFT FAIR
10AM, SATURDAY, NOVEMBER 30, 2019
OPEN TO THE PUBLIC
FORT RANDALL
CASINO • HOTEL

5TH ANNUAL FALL FLING
CRAFT & VENDOR SHOW

Saturday, November 2nd

10:00 A.M. - 2:00 P.M.

Dakota Christian School Gym

Over 40 vendor booths! Bake Sale! Soup & Sandwich Lunch

On your vendor application, request each vendor's **e-mail address**. Send group e-mails with any updates. Attach a sign about the craft fair and ask them to print and post copies if they live in different towns. Signs should be displayed wherever feasible. If allowed, vendors and committee members could put signs in workplace break rooms.

Save the e-mail vendors' addresses to notify them of future shows. Contact them *before* you advertise to give them first chance at being in your show.

If your community has a **local TV channel** with free or inexpensive area announcements, this is another opportunity to enlighten people about your event. Some **radio stations** invite area spokespersons to announce community events, so make sure that your craft fair is included.

Visit area craft fairs before your show and offer vendors applications to your event. That gives you a preview of their wares, and vendors feel good getting personal invitations.

When vendors pay their booth fees, part of that fee should go toward printed advertising. They expect and deserve it. Yes, it costs money, but everyone makes more money as a result.

Vendors need WiFi.

Multiple payment options mean more sales. Having good Internet service makes it much easier to run debit and credit cards.

If public WiFi isn't available, contact the facility's technology coordinator *in advance* to arrange for guest passwords or hotspots. Some sites, especially buildings with metal siding or roofs, have horrible reception.

If they have WiFi, vendors can share pictures of their booths on social media to attract visitors. A committee member could walk through the show while doing a Facebook live video of the booths.

Craft Fair
MASTER LIST

What to do &
when to do it!

DO NOT LOSE THIS
MANUAL!

Make a manual.

Start a binder with organizational information:

- committee members each year
- who did which jobs
- dates certain duties must be completed
- dates when tasks were completed
- an overview of the event
- considerations for future events

If you put the printed pages in clear sheet protectors, you can make photocopies or rearrange information as needed.

Think of wedding planners: "X" amount of months before the wedding, do this; "X" amount of weeks (or days) before the wedding, do that. Create a checkoff list for your wedding—I mean, craft fair.

The binder will become an invaluable resource, especially as committee members change over the years. Nobody can remember everything and having an organized to-do list relieves stress and improves events.

Who gets to keep the binder? The most organized member of the committee "wins" this task.

Another idea is to have a "cyber-binder" on a shared online storage program like Google Drive, Dropbox, or OneDrive. This way all committee members can view it and add notes. Still keep a printed copy as backup and as a scrapbook.

5 W's and 1 H

Just like a good journalism story, you need to determine the 5 W's and 1 H.

1. **Who:** Who is on your committee? Who will your vendors be? Who is your target customer base? VITAL: *Who will contact the state's **Department of Revenue** office about providing vendors with sales tax reporting sheets for your event?*

   Who else can assist with this event? The more people involved, the better the visibility. For example, any time you can include teenagers to help, their parents will know about the event.

   High school students have many talents and lots of energy. If the event is related to something that benefits them (music boosters, athletic boosters, after-prom party, school, park, library, etc.), their assistance is appropriate. Some teen groups need community service projects to fulfill certain goals.

   Students could
   - help set up the tables and chairs
   - open doors and help haul vendors' items
   - work at the concession stand (with adults)
   - take and deliver vendors' food orders
   - provide kids' story time, crafting lessons, or other activities in a designated area

2. **What**: Yes, it's a craft fair, but what could it be called to attract both vendors and customers? The terms *fall festival, spring fling, ladies' night out, vendor blender, harvest festival, holiday craft fair,* and *sip and shop* are used regularly. They're catchy names, and to make one of them "yours," just add your location or group's name.

    What type of show do you want? Determine your parameters. Will it be a mix of crafters and direct sales people? Will you allow vendors with flea-market items? May retail stores set up displays?

    What can you do to set your show apart? What traditions could you establish? One show in my area is known for its cheesy baked potato soup that the committee serves at its lunch stand. Some people come for the soup and then shop; others shop and then enjoy the "soup-er" meal.

    What other local events (organized by others) could be held on the same day? Ideas include

    - Tour of Homes or garden tours
    - Chamber of Commerce promotions
    - Town festival
    - Show & Shine car show
    - Citywide rummage sale
    - Farm show or implement open house
    - Gun show
    - Parade of Lights
    - Soup, pie, or barbecue cook-off

Chill Out in Delmont
Sunday, Nov. 21, 2021
10 am to 3 pm
Delmont Legion Hall

Christmas for everyone!
Warm Up With Food

Muffins & Coffee will be served starting at 10 am with homemade soups & a sandwich starting at 11 am.

KIDS ACTIVITIES

Paint a ceramic item, or make a gnome will be offered anytime during the event.

1 pm will have story time featuring ***children's book author Brenda DeHaan.***

Parents can join along in any event.

Hand crafted items only.

Sewn, crocheted, painted items, yard art, baked goods, wreaths, children's books, bird houses, note pads, photo albums, dish towels, kids tents and much more.

Join the fun, meet your neighbor, make a new friend, sit and visit over a roll & coffee or have some lunch.

All on the Main floor of the Legion Hall. Handicapped accessible with chair lift.

2	3	4					5	6	7				
9	10	11					12	13	14	15			
15	16	17	18				19	20	21	22			
22	23	24	25				26	27	28	29	30		
28	29	30	31										

FEBRUARY   AUGUST

					1							
3	4	5	6	7	8	2	3	4	5	6	7
10	11	12	13	14	15	9	10	11	12	13	14
17	18	19	20	21	22	16	17	18	19	20	21
24	25	26	27	28	29	$^{23}/_{30}$ $^{24}/_{31}$	25	26	27	28	

MARCH   SEPTEMBER

1	2	3	4	5	6	7		1	2	3	4	5
8	9	10	11	12	13	14	6	7	8	9	10	11	12
15	16	17	18	19	20	21	13	14	15	16	17	18	19
22	23	24	25	26	27	28	20	21	22	23	24	25	26
29	30	31					27	28	29	30

APRIL   OCTOBER

		1	2	3	4				1	2	3
5	6	7	8	9	10	11	4	5	6	7	8	9	10
12	13	14	15	16	17	18	11	12	13	14	15	16	17
19	20	21	22	23	24	25	18	19	20	21	22	23	24
26	27	28	29	30			25	26	27	28	29	30	31

MAY   NOVEMBER

				1	2	1	2	3	4	5	6
4	5	6	7	8	9	8	9	10	11	12	13
11	12	13	14	15	16	15	16	17	18	19	20
18	19	20	21	22	23	22	23	24	25	26	27
25	26	27	28	29	30	29	30

JUNE   DECEMBER

	3	4	5	6				1	2
10	11	12	13	6	7	8	9
17	18	19	20	13	14	15
25	26	27	20	21
			27

3. **When:** October-December are prime times, but craft fairs are held year-round. In the spring many people buy gifts for Easter, Mother's Day and graduation. When works the best for your committee? When will your venue have the best availability?

   Most craft fairs are scheduled the same weekend each year (like the second Saturday in November). Find out which annual events are held in your area because that will affect attendance.

   It's helpful to have at least two weeks between events in neighboring towns. Your target customer base will have a lot of overlap, and people will be more likely to attend events if they aren't back-to-back. If that's not possible, then be your area's first fair of the season.

   When will vendors be allowed to set up? If it works for them to set up the night before the event, then it's not as hectic during the hours before the show. Part of this depends on when the committee will have time to prepare the space.

   In some regions, hosts are expected to provide 6' or 8' tables and two chairs as part of the vendor fee; others require the vendors to bring their own tables and chairs or pay extra to have them provided. What amenities are expected in your area?

Booth spots must be determined in advance. If you provide tables and chairs, then you must set them up. Each vendor's business name must be put in the assigned booth space. You could put the sales tax form on each table then if that would streamline things.

If vendors cannot set up until the morning of the show, don't start the show until 10 a.m. For those who travel, they need time to reach the venue in addition to time setting up. Some vendors take 1-2 hours to unpack and prepare their displays. If the show starts at 9:00, they might have to leave so early from home that they won't want to do the show. Who wants to leave home at 6:30 a.m. on a Saturday?

What time do you need to arrive to welcome the vendors? When will you get any concessions ready?

When will the show end? In a small town, will most people have attended by 2:30-3:00? If your show is on a Sunday, wait until the afternoon to open.

A Ladies' Night Out event shouldn't start until vendors can get there from their day jobs. It is very helpful if vendors can set up the night before.

After the show, it might take vendors an hour to pack up. They need to clear their area before you can fully dismantle everything and leave the space as orderly as you found it. With all these considerations in mind, choose your show times after debating the variables.

4. **Where:** The less expensive the venue, the more profitable for the benefit. If you can incorporate school groups or if it's a benefit for a community cause, you may be able to use the school gym or community center for free or for a reduced rent.

   Where can you rent a large enough space to host at least 20 vendors? As an option to your school gym which may be too busy with school events, does your community have any buildings with large meeting rooms, such as a restaurant, VFW, American Legion, Armory, senior citizens' center, 4H center, or church?

   It is important to have a handicapped-accessible venue with sufficient parking.

   Will you need to purchase insurance for your event, or will you be included under the venue's policy?

   Do not book your event upstairs or in a lower level unless a large public elevator is available. Even then, do this only as a last resort because vendors must make numerous trips to haul everything in and out. People will be competing for elevator space, and they won't be happy. They might refuse to return to future shows.

   If your venue is near a movie theater, check if it would show a special children's movie during the craft show. They may agree show an older kids' film with free admission.

Conversely, schedule a Ladies' Night Out event on an evening when the movie theater is typically closed. Arrange for the theater to show a "chick-flick" and offer free wine. Only adult women may attend this special movie. It could even be a classic movie from 20 years ago.

On a wine theme, if a winery or micro-brewery is in your area, would they have room to host a craft fair? This would be a classic venue to "sip and shop." If it's a business that has a beer garden area, you could have a spring sip and shop event with the vendors inside but seating for lingering shoppers in the beer garden area. Free hors d'oeuvres could be available, so the vendors' booth fees would partially fund this expense.

Sometimes the "where" plays a role in attracting people to your craft fair.

5. **Why:** You are sponsoring this fundraiser to benefit others. Promote your cause.

- Why should people support it?

- Why is your show the best place to shop?

Make vendors and customers feel good about helping others. Explain your plans for the money.

Bonus benefit idea: In addition to fundraising for your organization, you could help others at the same time. One craft fair organizer was regularly asked how many guests attended her show. To get a crowd estimate, she started requesting that attendees donate either $1 for the food pantry or a non-perishable food item. She raised $1,000 for the food pantry and helped stock their shelves with more food. To do something similar, someone would need to be greet guests at the door and accept the donations.

Coordinating your show with a coat, hats, gloves, or mittens drive would help others stay warm in the winter and would warm the hearts of those who donated. People who may not have otherwise attended your show might stop by to deliver their donations and then stay to visit your vendors.

The craft fair could be a collection site and could "drive" attendance.

6. How: How is this all going to work, anyway?

- How much will your expenses be?

- How often will your committee meet? Do you have to meet in person or would periodic group e-mails, Zoom, or conference calls work?

- How much will you charge for the booth spaces? Booth fees may range from $25-$75 but might be over $100 for a large show attracting a huge crowd. Will a double booth cost less? Some charge $30 for a single booth or $50 for a double.

- How many booths will fit inside the venue?

- How much profit is reasonable to expect? If you have 25 booths at $25, the booth fees would total $625. If vendors would pay $30-$50, your total would increase to $750-$1,250. If you could secure a free or inexpensive venue, then the main expense would be advertising. Vendors would surely pay a little more for booth fees if the extra was dedicated to extensive advertising.

- How else can you raise money? Could you sell raffle tickets and/or run the concession stand?

- How are you going to accomplish everything? (First, keep reading. Next, don't forget that handy-dandy manual so you will remember how to do everything year after year.)

Preparations

You need vendors to have a craft fair. To find them, advertise in your area shopper and join relevant Facebook vendor groups where people post their shows and ask for vendors. To find groups, search on Facebook for "craft fair vendors in (my state)." From the results, select the most promising ones and ask to join them.

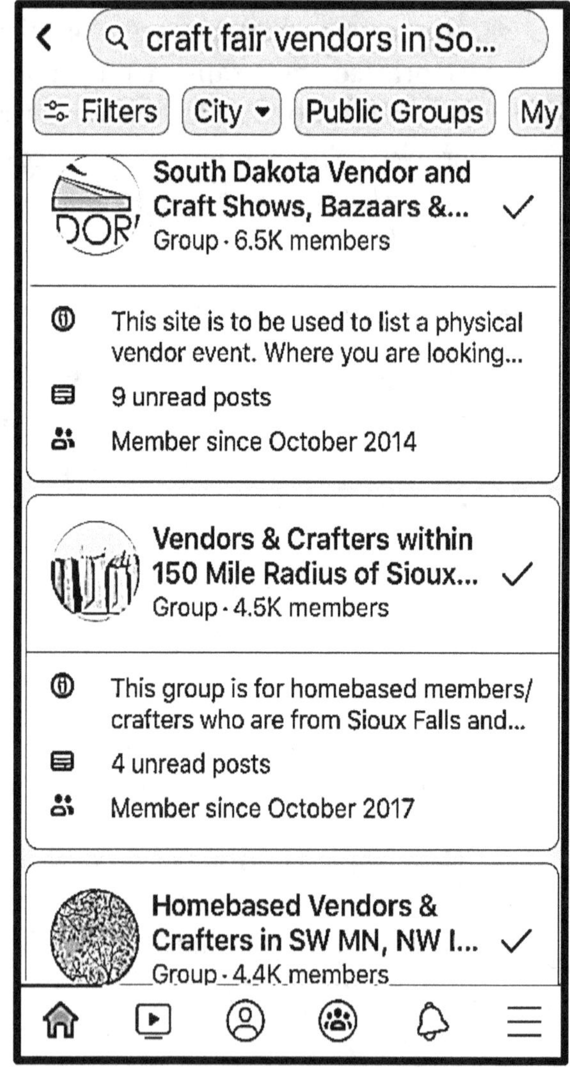

After becoming a member, you are allowed to post about your show and explain the type of vendors you'd prefer. Interested people can send you a private message to finalize contact details. Avoid publicly posting private e-mail addresses because scammers can cause difficulties.

Make sure that your vendor application includes exactly what the booth fee includes and other important information:

- the table size (6' or 8', if provided)
- the total booth space
- any additional cost if using electricity
- set up times
- consequences for leaving early
- if the vendor must donate a door prize
- the venue's street address and directions
- where to mail the application
- what name should be on the check
- whom to contact with questions
- application deadline
- where area motels are located, if applicable

Vendors are not your show's vendors until they have submitted applications and have *paid*. You need that financial commitment, or they could easily cancel at the last minute.

With direct sales companies, accept only the first one who pays the booth fee. Some may send the application form online but wait with the money. If they do that and another salesperson with the same product applies WITH payment, the paid application should win, but make that clear in your vendor information.

Make a layout design in pencil; many changes will be made, especially the first year in a venue.

You need to plan for how much space each vendor will have. For width, ten feet accommodates an 8' table with only a foot on each side for the vendor to get in and out. A common size is 10' x 10', but if your space allows for 12' wide booths, that would be better for the vendors and for traffic flow. Vendors value as much space as possible.

Check space requirements for ADA requirements and the fire marshal's guidelines. Search online for "ADA compliance for temporary events" for more information.

Some may bring extra tables or floor displays and might rearrange their areas to better accommodate their products.

If you have an inner rectangle of vendors and other vendors along the room's perimeter, people requiring electricity will need to be by the walls with outlets unless the venue has outlets on the floor. Inform vendors in advance to not use long extension and to tape all cords to the floor to prevent tripping.

Corner spots work well for double booths.

If the vendor sells clothing and doesn't have a pop-up dressing room, she will appreciate being closest to the bathroom for people who want to try on clothes.

Scatter the product types throughout the venue. For example, spread out the jewelry vendors; don't assign them all in the same row. If vendors selling similar types of items are next to each other, people may be confused about which items belong to which vendor. Also, those with scented products won't want to be next to another booth that also sells fragranced items. The smells could conflict with each other, and customers could have a difficult time determining which products they want.

Speaking of fragrances, be aware that some vendors and customers may be allergic to scented products. If certain areas have better ventilation, consider assigning those spots to vendors selling essential oils or other scented products. You don't have control over people's allergies, but if you can be sensitive to the situation, it could make a big difference for someone.

What attraction could you include to build buzz and lure kids to the show? Kids = parents = customers.

If applicable, have a designated time and area for kids to take pictures with Santa, the Easter Bunny, a Superhero or two, Disney characters, the school mascot, or any entity exciting to kids. The "special guest" could be available from 11-1 to give people enough time to take pictures, and that time slot will support the lunch stand.

The longer people linger, the more they will spend. If you have sufficient space to have a dining area near the vendors, people will stay longer. The longer they are there, the more products they will notice.

A craft fair can overwhelm people with its colorful array of products and prices. If they walk through the circuit more than once, they will focus on more items and will be better customers. Give them reasons to stick around.

If you have a raffle where people purchased tickets, you could require them to be present to win. The prizes could be donated from local businesses or could be purchased but sell enough tickets to make a nice profit. Prizes might be a quilt, ten turkeys (for 10 people), a sled, a patio set, a bicycle, a grill, a sleigh ride, a spa basket, etc. These prizes should be more enticing than the door prizes donated by the vendors.

You will need a sound system for making announcements and for playing music if you choose to do so.

Periodically empty the names in the drawing for the free door prizes. Announce when you do this so that if people are still present, they may sign their names again. Otherwise, at 2:00 you may be drawing names of people who left before 11:30. You want people to win prizes, so draw every 30 minutes when the people are likely to be there. People get excited when they win something.

Show Time!

Naturally, the more organized your preparations, the more smoothly your day will go.

Either in your application, your group e-mails or messages, or when you distribute the sales tax forms, ask vendors to move their vehicles after unloading so customers can access the venue more easily. After the customers have left, those closer parking spots will become available again.

In addition to the sales tax form, you could include an application for next year's show if you have already reserved the venue for the desired weekend.

Having large trash cans in every corner is helpful. Check them periodically to see if they need to be emptied.

Music adds a delightful ambiance, regardless of the season. After Thanksgiving, Christmas music motivates holiday shopping. Keep the music's volume where it is in the background, not so loud where it could be challenging for people to hear each other talk.

If the committee wears matching shirts or colors, this helps out-of-town vendors and guests to know who is in charge of the event. Name tags help also.

Treat your vendors well. You can't have a craft show without them. They could have gone to someone else's craft fair, but they picked yours. Make them rejoice in their choice.

During the show, someone from the committee should stop at the vendors' booth, ask how things are going, and thank them for coming to the show.

If the vendor brings young children who are going into other vendors' areas, a committee member should politely inform the responsible party that her children need to stay in her own area.

Offer free coffee to vendors throughout the day. At one craft fair, the organizers serve warm coffee cake to vendors before the show opens. Each year this fun show has more vendor requests than available booth spaces.

Vendors sell at a vast variety of shows throughout their crafting careers. Give them a comment card to get their feedback on what they liked about your show and any suggestions to make it even better next year.

Craft shows are positive, profitable events when managed well. Make yours be everybody's favorite show of the year!

GENERIC APPLICATION CONSIDERATIONS
(Adapt to fit your event.)

Name of event
Location
Date
Show times

Vendors, please keep this sheet for your records.

Application deadline:

Vendor registration fee:

Booth space dimensions:

Tables, chairs, and electricity details

Set up times

Booth must remain open during the entire show unless prior arrangements have been made.

Vendors are responsible for

Will food be available?

Will each vendor need to donate a door prize?

Committee contact information:

The committee is not responsible for injuries or stolen, lost, or damaged items.

Information for a separate sheet for vendor to mail or e-mail

Contact name

Business name

Tax ID number (if applicable)

Mailing address

Cell phone number

E-mail address

Description of products to be sold

Single space or double space (with each cost)

Is electricity needed? (All cords must be taped to the floor.)

Payment information

Payment must be sent with application to secure spot.

About the Author

In addition to being an author, Brenda DeHaan wire-wraps jewelry, is a K-12 librarian in two school districts, and loves being a grandma. She spends a lot of time straightening books on library shelves and straightening necklace chains at craft fairs.

She would be grateful for your brief review of this book.

Thank you for your support and interest.

Keep crafting!

A ***craft crawl*** is a different type of craft fair where the attendees travel to various locations. If you would like to try something different for your event, ***Craft Fair Q & A*** explains craft crawls in detail.

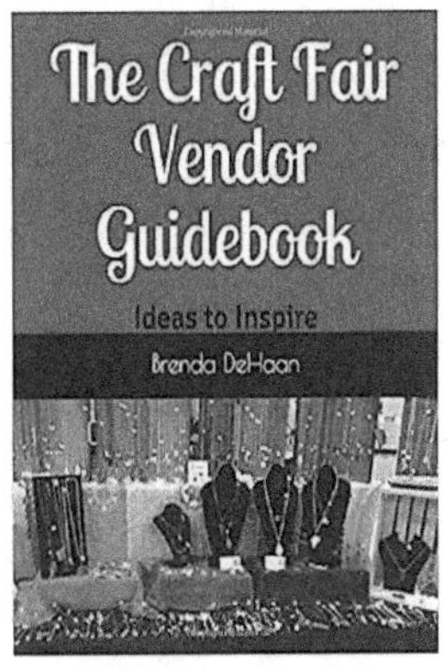

Please follow *Brenda DeHaan* on Amazon and *Brenda DeHaan, author* on Facebook and Instagram.

She hopes this book was helpful and invites you to read her other books.

Books "Crafted" by Brenda DeHaan

All books are available in paperback, most are enrolled
in Kindle Unlimited, and five have hardcover options.

Crafting

- ***Craft Fair Q & A:*** *From Craft Crawls to Quick Answers*
- ***Craft Fairs from A to Z***
- ***29 Tips for Craft Fair Vendors***
- ***Jewelry Vendors' Guidebook***
- ***Craft Fair Life***
- ***The Craft Fair Vendor Guidebook***
- ***Host a Successful Craft Fair***
- ***Crafty Decluttering***

Healing Crystals

- ***Rockin' Crystals***
- ***Crystal Haiku***
- ***Crystal Angel Affirmations***
- ***Wie Kristallengel ermutigen***
- ***Las Afirmaciones con los Ángeles de Piedras Preciosas***
- ***My Amethyst Journal***
- ***My Rose Quartz Journal***
- ***My Apache Tear Journal***

Writing

- ***Self-Publishing Painlessly for Free***

Children's Picture Books

- *Jasper Kitty Finds a Family*
- *Jasper Kitty Gives Little Dog Jumping Lessons*
- *Jasper Kitty Shares 17 Cat Tips*
- *Jasper Kitty Gets a Brother*
- *Rocks Rock*
- *ABC Amazing Book of Crystals*
- *Crystals for Kids*
- *The Flower Fairies Meet the Talking Rainbow Rocks*
- *Beach Surprise*
- *Hooray for a Fun Day!*
- *Rocks with Socks and Fox*
- *Rocks and Rhyme 2 in 1 Fun*
- *Adventures with Apollo*
- *Abenteuer mit Apollo*
- *Cat Naps, Dog Naps: Who Naps More?*
- *From Apple to Zombie Drawing Challenge:* Illustrate Your Own Halloween Book
- *From Angel to Zzzz's Drawing Challenge:* Illustrate Your Own Christmas Book

Tweens and Teens

- *Shine Life a Crystal:* 12 Quick Tips to Rock Life
- *Life Advice for Teens from an Ageless Grandma*